NLP M

*The 24 Neuro L   ogramming &
Mind Control Scripts That Will
Maximize Your Potential and Help You
Succeed in Anything*

© **Copyright 2015 - All rights reserved.**

This document is geared towards providing exact and reliable information in regards to the topic and issue covered. The publication is sold with the idea that the publisher is not required to render accounting, officially permitted, or otherwise, qualified services. If advice is necessary, legal or professional, a practiced individual in the profession should be ordered.

- From a Declaration of Principles which was accepted and approved equally by a Committee of the American Bar Association and a Committee of Publishers and Associations.

In no way is it legal to reproduce, duplicate, or transmit any part of this document in either electronic means or in printed format. Recording of this publication is strictly prohibited and any storage of this document is not allowed unless with written permission from the publisher. All rights reserved.

The information provided herein is stated to be truthful and consistent, in that any liability, in terms of inattention or otherwise, by any usage or abuse of any policies, processes, or directions contained within is the solitary and utter responsibility of the recipient reader. Under no circumstances will any legal responsibility or blame be held against the publisher for any reparation, damages, or monetary loss due to the information herein, either directly or indirectly.

Respective authors own all copyrights not held by the publisher.

The information herein is offered for informational purposes solely, and is universal as so. The presentation of the information is without contract or any type of guarantee assurance.

The trademarks that are used are without any consent, and the publication of the trademark is without permission or backing by the trademark owner. All trademarks and brands within this book are for clarifying purposes only and are the property of the owners themselves, not affiliated with this document.

Table of Contents

Introduction 4
1. You Deserve Success 5
2. You Have the Power to Change 7
3. Overcome the Fear of Failure 8
4. Patience is a Virtue 9
5. Feel Good about Yourself 10
6. Boosting Confidence 11
7. Staying Positive 12
8. Creating an "Organized" Environment 13
9. When You Feel You Don't Matter 14
10. When You Need to Re-Energize 15
11. When You Need to Rise above Challenges 16
12. How to Fight Stress 17
13. Be More Open to Receiving All the Good Things 18
14. How to be Grateful 19
15. Taking Charge of Your Weight 20
16. Kicking the Bad Habits 21
17. Overcoming Procrastination 22
18. Letting Go of Your Emotions 23
19. Mastering the Art of Negotiation 24
20. Improving Your Productivity 25
21. Letting Go of Self-Criticism 26
22. Accomplishing Your Goals 27
23. To Be More Assertive 28
24. Overcoming a Fear of Public Speaking 29
Conclusion 30

Introduction

Thank you for purchasing the book, *"NLP Master's Scriptbook"*.

Here you'll find 24 NLP and mind control scripts that can help improve your life drastically by maximizing your potential and helping you succeed in anything that you put your mind to. The scripts provided can serve as guides so that you can make your own script, which will be better suited to your specific needs and goals.

Everything starts from the mind; when you begin to think big, expect big things to happen in your life. It's not rocket science; when you are in control of your mind, you are in control of your life. The key to the success of the NLP scripts is in creating a positive mindset and maintaining that mindset through consistent use and practice of the scripts provided. Ultimately, only you can change the situations that you find yourself in, and only you can decide to take action on a day-to-day basis.

Therapists know the power of mind use therapies like CBT, DBT, and hypnotherapy to make a positive and lasting impact in the lives of their patients. NLP isn't just some "psycho-babble" as the critics would have you believe. This is tried and true science and has been proven to be effective over and over again.

There's no denying that change is inevitable. After all, it is the very nature of life. All you have to do is to embrace it. Make that change now!

I hope you enjoy and learn a lot from this book, but remember; only you can choose to take action and implement these scripts into your daily life. I can show you the door, but you must walk through it.

Good luck!

1. You Deserve Success

Today, you find yourself standing at a fork in the road. What do you choose – the path to success or the path to failure? Well, if you picked the former, don't expect a worry-free ride. But that's okay because challenges are there to make success sweeter.

Important note – Italicized lines enclosed in quotation marks are to be recited.

Now, we begin by learning a meditation technique to achieve Zen.

- Sit somewhere comfortable.
- Close your eyes. Take deep, slow breaths and begin counting from 10 to 1.
    - 10…Allow your body to relax.
    - 9…Begin to let go.
    - 8…See the number as you continue to go into relaxation.
    - 7…See it clearly and let go.
    - 6…You are relaxing deeply now.
    - 5…Take your time – deeper and deeper, your body is relaxed.
    - 4…Rid the mind of all outside noises.
    - 3…See the number and let it all go.
    - 2…You are going deeper and deeper.
    - 1…Finally, you are in deep relaxation.
- You are now in a state where your mind absorbs anything.
- See yourself on an imaginary screen in front of you. You see a successful person who is grateful for everything.
- You remain positive despite the challenges and your confidence level is high. You are in control of your own thoughts because you are aware that your thoughts will become your reality.

- You remain true to your goal. You know exactly what it is you want and you continue to see it clearly in your mind.
- *"I cannot wait to achieve my goals. I act and behave as a successful person does. I deserve success. I am open to change and I embrace it. My time has come!"*
- In a few moments, you will get out of this hypnotic state, 1, 2, 3, 4, 5.
- Your eyes begin to open and you feel better than before.

2. You Have the Power to Change

This is how you let go of the past so that you can have control over your future by effecting change in your life in the present moment.

- Begin by doing deep breathing techniques. Your muscles begin to relax. Your mind and body begins to relax, as your eyes grow heavy with every deep breath you take.

- See yourself wander to a stream. The water is clean and there are trees all around. This is a tranquil and serene place.

- You see yourself lying in the water and your body begins to float. Your entire weight is being supported by the water beneath you.

- *"I am safe. I am protected."*

- You hear the sounds of the waterfall as it comes into full view, and you see clear water splashing down.

- You go under the waterfall and you feel lighter than ever. You begin to see lights of different colors and they enter your skin. They are healing you right this moment. The water and the light are washing away and healing all the pains and disappointments of the past. You begin to let go.

- You begin to focus on what you have in front of you – a stream of water ready to take that journey with you.

- The waterfall lets you focus on the present moment. *"I believe that everything I do today will directly influence my future, so I will think only of positive thoughts."*

- *"I am now in control of my life."*

- As you emerge from the water, you are a different person. You begin to feel the power and energy that will drive you onward. You now have the power to take on your present to ensure that you have a better future.

3. Overcome the Fear of Failure

You will never become successful if you continuously nurture your fear of failure. This fear exists only in your mind and you can use your mind to overcome it. Don't let fear keep you from achieving what you are supposed to achieve. Release all your fears and begin to feel free to succeed.

- Take a deep breath. With each deep breath, your body begins to relax. Let go of the tension in your muscles.

- Now, close your eyes and continue to breathe deeply and slowly as possible. Your mind and body is now relaxed.

- See yourself wandering in an empty street. You look around and the street is empty. As you continue to walk, you notice how the structures around you look neglected. You see blank windows. Buildings have no signs. The place looks abandoned. It's a dark place.

- You look ahead and you cannot see the end of the road.

- The wind blows up the dust on the street. There's no place to hide and you are scared. You just stand there and wonder how you even got there.

- Instead of being afraid, you begin to think of happy thoughts as you sit. You begin to think about how happy you were when your mom first bought you your toy car. Then you remember how amazed you were when you first went to your first magic show.

- You begin to think only positive thoughts and then you begin to open your eyes. You are still there in the middle of an empty and dusty street, but this time you are not afraid.

- You know that this is not the destination you want, and it's not the destination you deserve. So you begin to walk straight ahead.

- You remain focused straight ahead. You push aside the fear. You continue to walk and as you quiet down your heavily beating heart with positive thoughts, you begin to see a bright new horizon.

- Slowly, you see yourself entering a different street – where everything is bright and sunny. You begin to see people walking, talking, and laughing. You look around and see offices and buildings bustling with people.

- You know this is where you should be and you are not afraid anymore.

4. Patience is a Virtue

Everything is a process. You need to work for your success. It doesn't happen overnight. Still, some people do not have the patience to wait.

- Get into the process of deep relaxation and breathing.

- "I am patient and I understand that only the present exists. The concepts of tomorrow and the past remain elusive."

- "I am patient. I let go of the past because it can never be relived. The future is still non-existent so I don't have to worry about it. The only thing that matters is what happens today."

- "I am patiently developing and creating my future with what I do and think today. In the meantime, I am enjoying every moment. There is no reason to be worried about the future."

- "I am patiently living in the present! Everything will come together, eventually!"

5. Feel Good about Yourself

When you feel good, you stay positive, and that's what you need if you want to attract success in your life.

- See yourself in a giant movie screen in front of you. See yourself clearly – the color of your clothes, your facial expression, what you are doing, and the scenery behind you. Make the details as vivid as possible.

- Now, imagine that your "screen self" is feeling good right at that moment. See the person you see on screen and your real self merging – now you have allowed your "real self" to feel good too.

- *"I deserve to feel good. I deserve this."*

- *"I feel wonderful. I have never been this happy. I am healthy. I feel relaxed. I feel calm. I am happy!"*

- Now, each time you feel down because of disappointments or stress you should go back to imagining yourself on the screen feeling good and merge your "two selves" together.

6. Boosting Confidence

It is easy to lose confidence when failures come but you can help yourself get past that. Each time you need a confidence boost, breathe deeply and let your imagination fly.

- Allow your mind to relax by taking slow deep breaths. Allow your body to let go of the tension and anxiety.

- See yourself on a movie screen in front of you. You have full control of your screen self.

- Imagine yourself in a situation where you want to feel more confident. See yourself clearly. For instance, you want to be confident when you pitch a project proposal to a group of potential clients. See yourself in front of the client. See the images clearly – what you are wearing, where you are standing, what you are doing, how your audience is reacting, and how they interact with you. Make the images as vivid as possible.

- *"I am okay. I am doing fine. I can nail this. I feel good about myself. I am confident of the work I've done for this project."*

- Reflect on what you've seen on the screen. Imagine it happening for real. Congratulate yourself for a job well done.

- *"I am a new person. I deserve to be happy. I deserve all the accolades. I am confident in my skills and in what I am capable of. I am great!"*

7. Staying Positive

It is sometimes hard to stay positive when faced with day-to-day challenges. Staying focused on positive thoughts is an integral part of each of the scripts in this book, but it can be difficult.

Understanding how the mind works is the key. If your body is a vessel, your mind is the captain that runs the ship. The thoughts that you focus on will determine where the ship will go. If you feed your mind with negativity, then you'll end up negative and afraid. If you nurture positivity, then you'll end up positive and happy. So what do you choose?

- Imagine your mind is a car that is running on empty. You need fuel to be able to go to your destination. Feeding your mind with positive fuel would help it work in a positive manner.

- Read thought-enlightening books. Watch a feel good movie or TV program. Listen to good music. Meditate. Go outdoors and bask in the sun. Play with kids or with your pet.

- Think about the things that make you happy – the sound of the laughter of your child, or maybe the taste of cake or ice cream – anything that gives you a reminder of being happy.

- *"It is a good day! I am happy. I think only positive thoughts. I feel great!"* Fuel your mind with positive words.

- Keep looking for things to feel positive about. Associate yourself with positive people. Bring with you a small book of positive quotes.

- *"I am happy and I feel great!"*

8. Creating an "Organized" Environment

Your mind is clear when you are organized and focused.

- Imagine yourself entering a home that is well organized – where everything has a place, where everything has a purpose, whether to add beauty or functionality.

- Hear yourself saying, *"This is exactly who I am. I am an organized person. I am capable of creating an environment similar to this."*

- You continue to explore the home and you feel the calmness it brings. *"I am an organized person and my environment reflects my own beauty and simplicity. I joyfully commit to set at least half an hour every day creating a calm and tranquil environment.*

9. When You Feel You Don't Matter

Some people belittle themselves, especially when they are poor or have no education. They feel that there's nothing they can do to improve their lives. If sometimes you feel that you do not matter, think again and let this exercise help you understand that you are worthy – just like everyone else.

Have you ever looked at the stars at night and wondered how they look all the same yet scientists have a name for some of them? Each one is different; like every human being is different. No two persons are the same; even twins have their differences.

- *"I am unique. There is no one exactly like me. I'm perfect just the way I am. I may have flaws but I also have my own strengths."*

- When people look down on you, it is a reflection of their behavior. Don't ever look down on yourself.

- If you remain poor, that is because you don't want to give yourself a fighting chance to improve your life.

- *"I have my own skills and I am using them to improve my own life."*

10. When You Need to Re-Energize

Your daily grind can drain you. It is important that you re-energize so you can get back to working your full potential again.

- Imagine walking on a beautiful sandy beach with pristine waters. Now as you walk further, you notice that it's almost sunset and you have reached a beautiful lagoon. As you watch the sun going down into the water, marvel at its beauty.

- Feel the water in the lagoon as you go in. The water is just waist deep and you sit down, and then you find yourself floating immediately.

- Feel yourself letting go as you float freely and feel your body begin to relax.

- You are now looking into the sky. It is nightfall now and the stars are shining brightly. The Milky Way comes into full view and you begin to feel your body floating away into the Milky Way. As you float deeper into the galaxy, you begin to feel energized and completely relaxed.

- You begin to float back into the lagoon. You are now feeling the cold water. You see yourself standing up and you feel rejuvenated.

- You walk back into the beach feeling fully rested.

- Looking back into the lagoon, you know that you can always go back to this place whenever you need to recharge.

11. When You Need to Rise above Challenges

Consider yourself half dead if you don't encounter the ups and downs of life. You can never fully appreciate the ups if you have not conquered the downs. When you face adversities and challenges, you have to fight through them and not fall so far into despair that you give up.

- See yourself in a situation with someone that you have had difficulty working with. Think about just one instance that you had a disagreement with him or her. If there are several people and situations that you can think of, set those aside for now. Just focus on one person and one event in each session.

- Imagine the scene unfolding – the person comes up to you and suddenly begins to bicker. As the person continues to berate you, imagine him/her continuously shrinking until he/she is about three inches tall. As he/she shrinks, his/her voice gradually becomes more and more inaudible.

- As the other person keeps on shrinking, see yourself growing taller and taller until you are standing above them. You have become so tall that your head almost reaches the clouds. Feel the fluffy clouds around you and see how blue the sky is.

- *"I feel wonderful. I can rise above it all. I am bigger than anybody who puts me down. I am bigger than my problems. I am bigger than any difficult situation I have to face."*

- You have taken control of the situation. You realize that you can do it and you will do it.

12. How to Fight Stress

While there may be many things to think of and worry about, you don't need to succumb to stress.

- *"Everything is working out fine. I remain calm. I remain positive."*

- Do you notice how it feels good to stay positive despite facing a mammoth of a task or a challenging situation? When you remain positive, you stay in control. You remain focused on the task at hand.

- When you continue to have a positive attitude, you can think clearly and you see the most appropriate solutions to every problem.

- *"I know that I can work through this. I am easily finding the solutions to my problems. I know exactly what to do; there is no reason to worry."*

- Focus on your breathing as you say these positive words. Handle stress by thinking positively and practicing deep breathing techniques.

- Notice how good that feels? Notice how a positive attitude can melt away stress and anxiety?

- Stay positive and melt the stress away.

13. Be More Open to Receiving All the Good Things

It is okay to expect only the good things in life. When you remain positive, you will attract more positivity into your life. Be open. You're like a newly-purchased computer – one that's still in the process of getting all essential programs installed.

- Think about positive thoughts. Reject thoughts of poverty, sickness, and sadness; instead replace them with thoughts about freely receiving abundance, good health, and happiness.

- It is okay to desire to be happy and to be wealthy.

- "I am open to the abundance that the universe has to offer. I am open to happiness. I am open to good health."

- "I attract wealth easily. I am a money magnet. I remain healthy and happy."

- "Money, good health, and happiness are flowing freely into my life and I am giving it out to the world."

14. How to be Grateful

Having the attitude of gratitude keeps the good things coming in. When you remain thankful for all the things that you receive, they will keep on coming.

- See yourself up on a mountain. Look at the magnificent view. Look at the beauty of the world around you. You are atop the highest peak and clouds are all over. You step onto one of the fluffy clouds and it takes you to a wonderful place where you find peace and complete calmness.

- As the cloud transports you, feel your body relaxing deeply. You are now sinking into the calmness of the beautiful place the cloud has brought you.

- You feel the gentle breeze and the warmth of the sun on your skin.

- *"I am grateful for this beautiful place. I am grateful for having been able to experience this. I am grateful for being in this place right now. I am grateful for everything that I see around me. I am grateful for the peace and tranquility I am experiencing right now."*

- As you marvel at nature's beauty, think about the good things that you have in your life. Think about your family, your work, your business, your friends, your house, your car, and all the good things you can think of.

- *"I am grateful for the gift of life. I am thankful for my family."* As you go on enumerating the wonderful things you have in your life, feel it into your being. Recite everything that you are most thankful for. Feel the joy of being grateful for everything that you have in your life.

15. Taking Charge of Your Weight

Part of feeling good is looking good, plus, it is never healthy to be overweight. If you want to lead a healthy lifestyle, you have to begin with losing weight.

- Give yourself a pat on the shoulder for finally deciding to change your life and your physical appearance.

- Picture yourself walking into the park in your neighborhood. There are other people all around and they cannot help but look admiringly at you. Your friends take notice of how great you look.

- As you continue to walk, you feel lighter and you're bursting with energy. You feel wonderful in your new body. As you go back to the house, you catch a glimpse of yourself in a glass window.

- *"I am fit. I am healthy. I love the way my body looks now. I am vibrant. I am happy. I feel great!"*

- From this moment forward, you have to commit yourself to changing your eating habits and becoming more physically active.

16. Kicking the Bad Habits

If you want to improve your life, you have to learn to stop your bad habits. For instance, if you wish to lead a healthy lifestyle, you have to quit smoking.

- Practice deep and slow breathing until your whole body is relaxed.

- Think about the bad habit that you want to break. If there are several habits that you want to overcome, do it one a time. If you want to quit smoking, do it first.

- *"I will quit smoking starting today. I want to lead a healthy lifestyle. I am positive that I will kick this habit in no time."*

- See yourself throwing away packs of cigarettes in your drawer.

- *"I am better off without these. I am healthy. I am stronger. I am happier! I feel great!"*

17. Overcoming Procrastination

Some people think that they have unlimited time to complete a project of meet a deadline so they slack away until they have to cram. Overcome procrastination and avoid stressing out cramming to complete a project.

- For fear of failing or being criticized, some people tend to put off doing things until it is the "best time". Overcome this fear by thinking about your abilities. Find confidence. You were assigned that project because your boss knows you can do it.

- Think about the time that you first submitted a project and your boss commended you for it.

- Allow your mind to see you in your daily routine. See yourself determined to finish the task at hand. Reframe your mind. Take control.

- "I am finishing this project now. I have all the things that I need to finish this now. I will not slack off and I will not disappoint my boss. I am good at what I do. I am never late. I am great!"

- You have the power to change. Change your frame of mind. Do it now!

18. Letting Go of Your Emotions

There are moments when you become too emotional for your own good, especially during a time when you need to firmly decide on something.

- Practice deep and slow breathing. Feel your body relaxing.

- Be aware of your feelings. Think about the issue at hand. You need to decide on something but you cannot think objectively because your good judgment is being clouded by your emotions.

- Continue to relax but get in touch with that feeling.

- *"I am afraid of making the wrong decision."*

- Acknowledge that feeling.

- Now see yourself drifting into a dark room, bringing that negative emotion with you. See yourself go deeper and deeper into the dark. Understand why you are feeling that way. Search within you to find the source of that fear.

- Then, feel your body floating away from the dark room but leaving the negative emotion behind. Feel your body going into a brighter room feeling more relaxed.

- You can see clearly now. You have just released that negative emotion of fear and you are now ready to make a huge decision.

- *"I am calm! I am relaxed. I feel great!"*

19. Mastering the Art of Negotiation

If you want to effectively communicate and negotiate with other people, you need a lot of patience and understanding. In meetings and discussions, it is inevitable to have disagreements but neither side is necessarily right or wrong. They just have their own beliefs. You have the power to rise above any kind of situation. Let them speak and do not force your ideas on other people. Understand and listen. Have an open mind.

- *"I am open to the opinion of others. I understand where they are coming from and I am willing to listen. I already know my ideas and it's time to learn theirs."*

- "Negotiate" a solution that everyone can work with, act from a position of power – the power of knowledge. Ask questions and understand their views. When you keep asking questions, you take control.

- When they are finished speaking, repeat what they said to make sure that you understood and then share your ideas, taking into consideration their ideas.

- You are still in control but you have made other people believe that they, too, have a say in the decision-making.

- Having been able to exercise patience and being open-minded, you can negotiate from the "position of knowledge". This is how you can sway other people to implement your ideas without being overbearing. You are in control. Be patient.

20. Improving Your Productivity

When you are productive, you get more work done, thus your superiors will continue to trust you with projects. You have to learn to shut off distractions so you remain focused on the task at hand.

- When you have reached a state of relaxation, see yourself on your desk working on a project.

- See yourself focused, yet happy and calm.

- "I am productive. Though I have tons of work to do, I will not panic; I'll do things one at a time until I've completed them all. I start with the most difficult and important one. I will stop for short breaks but I won't let my mind get distracted. I am happily working on my tasks and I feel good about it."

21. Letting Go of Self-Criticism

It is common for most people to be highly critical of themselves. But you have to understand that nobody's perfect and everyone makes mistakes. You have to learn from your mistakes and then move on.

- Close your eyes and go back to a time when you were overly critical of something wrong that you did. Instead of beating yourself up for making a mistake, accept it and learn from it; and then let it go.

- Now, see yourself taking on a new project and completing it without a hitch.

- Let go of self-criticism; embrace your weaknesses and enhance your strengths.

- *"I am positive. I made a mistake but I have learned from it and now I am moving on."*

22. Accomplishing Your Goals

Believe that you can achieve anything. You cannot set limitations on what you can do.

- Focus on your goals. You should never lose sight of your hopes and dreams.
- When you remain focused, you won't settle for anything less.
- Change your frame of mind and stay positive.
- "By this time next year, I have already built my dream house. My family and I are living comfortably in that dream house."
- "I can accomplish anything I set my mind into. I am a winner and I am worthy of getting everything this universe has to offer. I may fail but I will rise again. I will use the challenges that come my way as stepping stones to achieving my goals."
- Beginning today, you have to believe that you can achieve anything.

23. To Be More Assertive

Your ideas matter; don't let people tell you otherwise.

- Just because you are not the boss, does not mean your ideas don't matter. Just because you are not well educated, does not mean you cannot accomplish anything.

- Don't belittle yourself. If you do, you will never accomplish anything. Always give 100% when you perform your job, not because you are somebody important, but because you are, you and you are capable.

- *"I am capable like everybody else. I am never afraid of voicing out my opinions and sharing my ideas. I am excited to learn new things. I impress people with what I can do. I am a leader!"*

24. Overcoming a Fear of Public Speaking

One of the most common phobias is the fear of speaking in public. People fail because they let fear take the better of them. It is natural to feel nervous every time you need to speak in public. However, if you did the necessary readings and preparations, there is no point in being anxious. These words will also help:

- *"I am confident in my abilities. I believe in myself. People love me."*

- *"People find me warm and friendly. They are drawn to me. They respond to me because I am a person with integrity. They enjoy my company."*

- *"When I get up and speak in front of people, they feel my warmth and they listen to me. I stand in front of people, poised and calm. I speak spontaneously. I am confident with the way I deliver my lines. When I speak, people listen because I speak with authority and conviction."*

Conclusion

Thank you for purchasing this book.

I hope you have taken to the scripts to heart; it will completely turn your life around.

The challenge now is to practice what you have learned and don't forget to share it with your family and friends.

Thank you and good luck!

Don't miss the next book in the series!

"NLP Master's Handbook: The 21 Neuro Linguistic Programming and Mind Control Techniques that Will Change Your Mind and Life Forever"

Keep reading for a sneak peek!

Chapter 2 – Basic NLP Techniques

There are a variety of NLP techniques that you can use for a host of different purposes. Every technique can be used by itself or combined with other techniques in order to create a new mindset that will be able to change your life forever.

Basically, there are 8 commonly recognized techniques:

#1 Anchoring

Anchoring induces a particular frame of mind or an emotion, like happiness, sadness, or relaxation. It often involves a gesture or touch, or something that you can identify as an *anchor* – it's like a "bookmark" for a particular emotion.

How does it work?

Go back to a time when you experienced overwhelming happiness, like when your child was born, when you won an award, or when you received your first paycheck. It could be anything that you have fond memories of.

In your head, think of the events that transpired leading you to that happy moment. Make the images more vivid. Think about how you felt during that time. Create a clear image of that moment and feel the emotions you had back then.

Next, hold your left index and your middle fingers with your right hand. Gently squeeze your fingers twice. As you squeeze them the second time around, recall the image of that happy moment, only this time, making the picture larger and happening close to you. Remember how happy you felt and feel that intense emotion starting to break free as it multiplies.

Describe how you're feeling again and what you were thinking then, do these while you squeeze your fingers again, twice. As you squeeze the second the feelings you described doubles. Let the feeling envelop your whole being. Feel it.

This is anchoring, each time you make squeezing actions to your fingers; you will be transported back to that time of overwhelming happiness. That particular action sends a signal to your brain to associate it with feelings of happiness.

#2 Pattern Interruptions

This NLP technique is more commonly used to store keywords to your listener's subconscious mind. Pattern interruption is best combined with other NLP techniques, particularly anchoring.

What is it?

Pattern interruption lures your listener's inner monologue or pure subconscious train of thought to establish a pattern.

Take this analogy. There is a boy who gets his pet dog to perform all of his movements for him. The boy is your conscious mind, while the dog represents your subconscious mind. The boy (conscious mind) makes all the decisions, and the dog (subconscious mind) performs all the actions that needed to be done.

Here's where the exercise begins. Ask the boy to make a sandwich. The boy then tells the dog to get the bread, slice the cheese, and place it on a plate. The boy then tells the dog to bring the food to a friend sitting right behind the shadow.

So, you ask the boy that you wanted another sandwich, so he gives his dog a similar sequence of command. The pet dog promptly gets the bread and cheese and places it on a plate.

Then, *"slap"* anyone who is near you. Next, slap the boy in the face and instruct him to dance. Before the dog can finish the final command during the sandwich test was interrupted, new commands have been given.

The boy who is the conscious mind, being depicted here as someone who is less clever, forgets that the sandwich is still not "delivered". However, the pet dog has not forgotten about the sandwich. Though the dog has no capacity to speak to the boy, he is thinking when the command for the sandwich will be given. That thought will stay with the dog for quite some time until he is told to fetch that sandwich.

You can easily tell the boy to give you his wallet. It is easy since the boy might ask his pet dog to bring the wallet to you. It is possible that the dog will bring you the wallet.

This is the perfect example of pattern interruption. This example may not work all the time but this particular technique is powerful.

To continue reading, visit the following link in your web browser:
http://www.books4everyone.com/nlp

Printed in Great Britain
by Amazon